THE FUTURE CITY

Lannoo

Foreword

by Ben van Berkel,
Founder and Principal Architect, UNStudio

Cities are the perfect example of what we can achieve if we act as a society, rather than as individuals. They are therefore also a celebration of our achievements as humanity. Over time, what has made people come together to live in dense populations is a simple case of cause and effect. With the evolution of settlements to villages, then to towns and cities, both the causes and the effects have expanded to become extremely complex networks.

To create a successful city, there needs to be a balance between intelligent planning, high-quality architecture and good infrastructure. Complexity needs to be managed through participation, analysis, knowledge and innovative strategies. This does not entail a solution-based practice such as engineering, but rather a strategic design approach. Of course, the true beauty of the city is that it is an ongoing process that keeps adapting, changing, decaying and renewing.

A great benefit of having many international projects is that I have been able to visit cities around the world that I might otherwise not have seen. When I travel, I try to take a day off to walk around and learn from these cities. They have often given me inspiration and new ideas. When designing for the urban context, I feel that recently people have become the central focus, as opposed to cars in the past. This was greatly aided by our early computational skills, which have now developed into tools that enable us to put the user experience first.

If cities are to continue to thrive while meeting the needs of a growing urban population, we need to make them more sustainable and healthier, both for the sake of people and the planet. I mean not only people's physical health, but also their social and mental health. We need to curate the growth very carefully and listen more to the community; involve it in early decision-making stages.

Perhaps the greatest challenge for cities today is the equitable distribution of resources, such as access to green space, work, education and social mobility. We need to pay particular attention to local public space and access to green space in cities, and we must use technology to build an interactive relationship with citizens. We also need to prepare for the climate crisis that is upon us with nature-inclusive design.

Technology has a role to play in the future city, but we need to create the right tools to bring people together. Not surveillance tools, or tools that simply improve efficiency, but rather data analysis that is more user focused and personal. This means that in our profession we need more specialised people and more specialised artificial intelligence. Advances in energy technology will also revolutionise the way we live and travel. This is why I founded UNSense, our sister arch-tech company, to work with technologies that can support how we plan and serve our cities and their inhabitants in the future.

Looking ahead, I think the main changes to our cities will not necessarily be very easy to spot. It will be less about how they will look and more about how they will behave. I can imagine a proliferation of new technologies that will merge our digital and physical worlds. Buildings will behave as a kind of software, with increased flexibility and circularity of construction parts and materials. I can also imagine that the time between idea and building will be compressed and that there will be a rapid prototyping of the city. I also think we can expect a lot more green, more nature, both cultivated (in the form of urban farming) and wild, as well as the use of more natural materials in our buildings.

In the end, we are all urban creatures, social-technical beings, but in the city we can also choose anonymity; we can decide when we wish, or need, to be part of the group, and when we want to withdraw and enjoy the privacy of the family unit; the safety and isolation of the home. Principally, alongside convenience and employment, cities offer an intensity of life that spurs creativity and inspiration derived from different people coming together. Cities also provide a sense of belonging that in the end drives us to safeguard them in return.

1.

Introduction

More than half of the world's population currently lives in cities, and another 2.5 billion citizens are expected to join them by 2050.[1] The United Nations (UN) predicts that nearly all population growth up to 2030 will be in cities, with 96 per cent of this increase occurring in Asia and Africa.[2] This incredible surge in the urban population demands that we urgently re-evaluate how cities are designed and built to best meet the needs of future inhabitants.

Cities have tended to evolve gradually in response to incremental changes in their population, density, wealth, trading opportunities and availability of resources, as well as to trends related to lifestyle choices, affordability, transportation, infrastructure, education and safety. In recent decades, however, many conurbations have developed at breakneck speeds as people gravitate to places experiencing booms in trade, commerce and industry.

The rate at which cities are growing presents numerous challenges for stakeholders involved with urban development. The following are just some of the many complex questions that planners, policymakers and designers are required to address. How can established metropolises continue to expand while offering the same quality of life to all future inhabitants? Can we quickly create new districts or entire cities to successfully accommodate increasing numbers of urbanites? How might new technologies make city living smarter and more efficient? And how can we achieve all of this while preventing further damage to our planet's fragile ecosystem?

---

1 United Nations, Department of Economic and Social Affairs, Population Division, *World Urbanisation Prospects: The 2018 Revision.*

2 UN-Habitat, *World Cities Report 2020: The Value of Sustainable Urbanization.*

Architects, designers, engineers and urban planners have a vital part to play in creating the next generation of urban environments. Working in collaboration with national and local governments, developers and service providers, as well as with the residents who will ultimately occupy these future cities, they generate proposals that aim to meet the needs of citizens in innovative and sustainable ways. Only by responding creatively to the shifting political, economic, social and technological factors that affect how cities operate and evolve will we be able to ensure these places are fit for purpose, both now and for decades to come.

This book compiles a selection of radical, innovative and inspirational ideas for urban development, as envisioned by some of the world's leading creatives and future-focused companies. These pioneering concepts are organised into five sections, with each section representing an area of focus for those involved in the development of future cities: Masterplans and Megacities; Transportation and Infrastructure; Green Architecture and Urban Farms; Smart Cities; and New Habitats. Projects were chosen to represent unique approaches to the various themes, as well as to cover different geographical regions and provide inspiration for those interested in both the near and distant future of urban habitation.

The case studies include recently completed projects that embody ideas likely to influence how cities evolve in the coming years, along with speculative proposals based on emerging technologies or societal and technological trends. Some of the featured projects are unlikely ever to be built due to political, technical, logistical or bureaucratic obstacles. Others were never intended to be realised, as their main purpose is to provoke discussion about the sort of world we might wish to inhabit. Many of the case studies, however, are projects that are at an advanced planning stage or are currently under construction, and therefore offer a genuine insight into what the future city may look like and how it may function.

Urbanisation: a problem or a solution?

According to a 2018 UN report titled 'World Urbanisation Prospects', the world's urban population grew more than fourfold in the latter half of the twentieth and early years of the twenty-first centuries, increasing from an estimated 0.8 billion in 1950 to around 4.2 billion in the year of the report's publication.[3] The report stated that, as a result of this rapid urbanisation, in 2007 the population of the world became more urban than rural for the first time. It also claimed that: 'The urbanisation process is expected to continue for decades and an ever-increasing majority of humankind will likely be living in urban areas.'

For most of human history, however, the majority of people lived in small communities in more rural areas. The surge in urbanisation that has occurred in the past two centuries – and particularly in recent decades – has drastically reshaped the built environment, causing cities to spread and in some places merge to form vast urban agglomerations. This process has wide-ranging social, economic and cultural implications, including changes in dominant occupations, lifestyles and behaviours.[4]

The appeal of cities remains much the same today as it always has. Citizens can expect better job opportunities and higher incomes, while businesses benefit from

3 United Nations, Department of Economic and Social Affairs, Population Division, *World Urbanisation Prospects 2018: Highlights (ST/ESA/SER.A/421)*, 2019.
4 Ibid.

reduced costs, better infrastructure and improved opportunities for collaboration. However, the problems associated with urbanisation have also remained remarkably consistent as it has spread throughout the world. These include economic disorder, civil unrest, congestion and environmental degradation, as well as the proliferation of slums.

If urban sprawl is allowed to continue unchecked, it could lead to increasing numbers of people living in poorly designed, informal settlements with substandard sanitation, worsening air pollution and inadequate access to food and basic healthcare. The 2030 Agenda for Sustainable Development outlines the importance of successfully managing growth, especially in the 'developing world', which is predicted to account for 95 per cent of urban growth in the coming decades.[5] One of its goals is to work with local authorities and communities to renew and plan cities to make them better places to live, and to minimise their impact on the global climate system.[6]

In the coming years, cities will have a vital role to play in mitigating environmental threats and responding to climate change. Urban areas already consume two-thirds of the world's energy and generate 70 per cent of global carbon emissions,[7] so they must urgently begin to implement and adopt policies aimed at enhancing resource efficiency and reducing their per-capita environmental impact. Rapid urbanisation is also exerting pressure on freshwater supplies and sewerage, as well as the quality of the environment and public health. These trends need to be addressed at a policy and planning level to ensure the world's increasingly urban population is contributing to an overall pattern of progress and improvement in living standards.

---

5 Ibid.

6 UN General Assembly, *Transforming Our World: The 2030 Agenda for Sustainable Development*, 21 October 2015, A/RES/70/1.

7 UN-Habitat, *World Cities Report* 2020.

The New Urban Agenda, adopted at a UN conference on housing and sustainable development held in Quito, Ecuador, in 2016, sets out standards and principles for the planning, construction, development, management and improvement of urban areas.[8] It provides a framework for how well-planned and well-managed urbanisation can help to accelerate the UN's Sustainable Development Goals (SDGs), with a particular focus on Goal 11 – 'Make cities and human settlements inclusive, safe, resilient and sustainable'. The principles and ideas it proposes should be at the forefront of all future urban development in order to address the unique challenges resulting from urbanisation in different regions across the globe.

Influential architects

People have always been preoccupied with trying to envision what future civilisations might look like or how they might live. Fantastical versions of future cities feature prominently in some of the most popular science fiction writing, comic books, television programmes and films. From Jules Verne's prophetic descriptions of advanced transportation and communication technologies, to the stylised city presented in Fritz Lang's film *Metropolis* (1927) and Ridley Scott's dystopian version of the future Los Angeles in *Blade Runner* (1982), visions of future cities are now ingrained in popular culture.

Many of the world's great architects have also dedicated time to speculating about the future of urban living and how best to apply radical social, technological or creative concepts in an urban context. These ideas are used as the basis for manifestoes that inform their own practice, or to stimulate conversations about how we might wish to live in the future. Le Corbusier's influential 1929

8 United Nations, *New Urban Agenda*, 2016.

publication *The City of Tomorrow and Its Planning* outlined plans to move away from traditional models of urban planning and create more efficient cities based on skyscrapers set within large open spaces. The Swiss architect subsequently applied some of these ideas in large-scale projects in Marseille, France, and Chandigarh, India, among other cities.

The work of the architect and futurist Richard Buckminster Fuller in the middle of the twentieth century influenced many subsequent visions for urban design based on his unique experiments in the fields of science, engineering and sustainability. Fuller's work certainly inspired the UK-based art and architecture collective Archigram, which developed numerous provocative habitation concepts in the 1960s and 1970s. Its extreme proposals included the Walking City, which would move on giant legs to a suitable location, and the Plug-In City, featuring modular units that form a constantly evolving megastructure.

Other important figures active in the field of urban architecture in the twentieth century include pioneers of the Metabolist movement such as Kenzō Tange and Kisho Kurokawa; Estonian American architect, professor and critic Louis Kahn; Moshe Safdie; Oscar Niemeyer; and Alison and Peter Smithson, whose 'New Brutalism' influenced the design of many post-war cities in Britain and around the world. More recently, Dutch architect, urbanist and theorist Rem Koolhaas has produced numerous influential projects and publications examining the role of the city in modern society. Danish architect Bjarke Ingels, whose eponymous studio, BIG, features several times in this book, is another influential figure who has claimed that a masterplan for the Earth is required to help holistically tackle the environmental issues facing society in the future. These names represent a small sample of the progressive thinkers and practitioners that have helped to shape the evolution of cities thus far, with many more working diligently on more practical, everyday applications of architecture in the creation of successful urban spaces.

The projects compiled in this publication represent a selection of ideas from some of the most influential architects and firms practising today. The book's length and the formatting of the sections mean that many familiar and important names are not included, but nevertheless the case studies seek to provide a compelling insight into the minds of some truly innovative thinkers working to create the cities of today and tomorrow.

Visionary visualisations

The techniques used by architects and designers to present ideas about future cities have reached unprecedented levels of sophistication and hyperreality in recent years. Advances in computing software enable these professionals, along with visualisation specialists, to produce rendered images that depict in exceptional detail their designs for cities, buildings or infrastructure systems. The quality of these digital visualisations is one of the main reasons for producing this book at this particular moment in time, as they enable a wide array of projects from both established and emerging architectural practices to be presented in a visually rich and engaging format.

Of course, high-quality renderings are more typically used by architects, developers and their public relations departments as a tool to present early ideas to the public, their peers and potential investors. They may not accurately represent the final outcome, or even be practicable in reality, but increasingly they can help to communicate proposals in a compelling and believable format. Each case study in this book was chosen because of the strength of its central idea and its relevance to one of the five chosen topics. To maintain a level of visual consistency, only projects with suitably high-quality imagery have been used. This means some potentially relevant projects have missed out, but hopefully the final selection delivers an overview that is cohesive, comprehensive and engaging enough to inspire and inform.

The future city

Most of the projects presented in this book are designed to meet the challenges currently facing urban populations, or to combat issues that could affect citizens in the next two or three decades. Looking this far into the future, we can be confident that cities will not look radically different from how they do today, as the evolution of construction technologies and aesthetic styles in urban architecture is typically fairly slow. A gradual process of development will see new buildings layered alongside their predecessors to form heterogenous urban environments. The visible transformation of cities will also be mitigated by the increasingly common act of adapting existing buildings in an effort to reduce the economic and environmental costs associated with new construction.

Current social, technological and environmental trends can also help us to identify likely future directions for urban development. In particular, the importance of well-being and the increasing focus on sustainability will guide the policy decisions of city planners, as well as the lifestyle choices of their inhabitants. The majority of planned development in the coming years will focus on improving liveability and sustainability. Mixed-use buildings designed as vertical neighbourhoods will incorporate workspaces, living accommodation and leisure facilities, providing all essential amenities within a short walking distance to reduce the need for transit. Where transportation is required, it will mostly be shared, autonomous and non-polluting. Green spaces will become more common as municipalities seek to support citizens' physical and psychological well-being. Technology will also become increasingly important as we become more used to living with artificial intelligence, smart infrastructure and connected devices. These technologies will use sensors to gather information about our needs and behaviours, which will be used to control energy systems, buildings and industries to enhance how we live and work. In summary, we can expect cities to steadily become smarter, cleaner, greener and better connected – both physically and digitally.

Looking even further ahead, the pace at which technologies are evolving could allow humankind to begin colonising new habitats within our lifetimes. Scientists, engineers and architects are already developing proposals for communities that float on the ocean's surface or are submerged in its depths. Recent advances in space exploration have raised the possibility of whether we could build cities on Mars or the Moon. Some of the concepts detailed in the New Habitats section of this book (page 156) might seem radical today, but they are based on scientific research and technologies that are already in development. Only a century ago, it would have seemed unlikely that a human being would one day walk on the Moon, or that we would be able to construct buildings a kilometre in height. If we can successfully apply humankind's capacity for innovation, the future city can be whatever we want it to be.

2.

By 2030 the world is projected to have at least 43 megacities – defined as having more than ten million inhabitants.[1] The majority of these will be located in developing regions, with Delhi predicted to become the most populous city in the world around 2028.[2] However, some of the fastest-growing cities will be those with fewer than one million citizens, many of which

1 United Nations, Department of Economic and Social Affairs, Population Division, *The World's Cities in 2018 – Data Booklet* (ST/ESA/ SER.A/417), 2018.

2 United Nations, Department of Economic and Social Affairs, Population Division, *World Urbanisation Prospects 2018: Highlights* (ST/ESA/SER.A/421), 2019.

and

Masterplans

will be in Asia and Africa.[3] Both megacities and smaller urban settlements present opportunities for supporting people out of poverty by providing better housing, education, healthcare and employment. However, if not regulated properly, urban spread can result in increasing numbers of people living in overcrowded slums or shanty towns with high rates of disease, malnutrition and a lack of basic healthcare.

3 Ibid.

Megacities

The mass migration of people from rural to urban areas in recent decades has prompted the construction of many new cities and neighbourhoods from the ground up. In areas where growth is allowed to occur unchecked, or development is primarily focused on profit, these urban districts can end up being unattractive, disjointed and poorly integrated with existing neighbourhoods. The process known as masterplanning aims to address these issues by setting out a proposal for future growth and development. The best masterplans consider how architecture, infrastructure, services and governance can combine to deliver a liveable, successful and sustainable environment for generations to come.

Planning a new city or urban district is a complex, expensive and risky undertaking, fraught with political and logistical challenges that can easily dilute the original vision or bring a halt to it altogether. The task of creating masterplans is typically entrusted to some of the world's biggest architectural firms. Working alongside teams of developers, planners and engineers, as well as specialists in infrastructure and landscape design, these agencies produce concepts that guide all future construction.

The projects represented in this section display diverse approaches to masterplanning new urban settlements. The differences between them are a consequence of their geography, climate, anticipated population or unique future vision. Masterplans such as these are often created to test a development's feasibility and core principles before a more detailed planning phase is undertaken. For this reason they can afford to be more conceptually bold and future-focused than the eventual built outcome.

The selection of projects included here aims to cover different geographical regions and includes visions for new cities along with redeveloped sites in existing urban centres. The chapter could easily have been filled exclusively with projects from China, as the country has produced dozens of masterplans over recent years aimed at accommodating its rapidly urbanising population. Some of these never leave the drawing board, while others fail to deliver on their promises of a high-tech, prosperous urban utopia. However, the completion of the Nanjing Zendai Himalayas Center designed by MAD Architects (page 34) demonstrates that China is capable of successfully delivering visionary masterplans when they are properly designed, funded and managed.

This chapter also features projects in Europe that demonstrate new approaches to the development of green belt land and the repurposing of existing urban districts to meet the changing needs of their inhabitants. Meanwhile, in Africa, Skidmore, Owings & Merrill's masterplan for a new community near Nigeria's capital, Abuja (page 46), could provide a much-needed blueprint for sustainable urban development in Africa.

The majority of the megacities projected to exist in ten years' time will have evolved organically and without a cohesive masterplan. Without involvement from urban designers, architects and planners, many of them will struggle to meet the targets laid out in the UN's 2030 Agenda for Sustainable Development. These include such crucial points as access for all to adequate, safe and affordable housing, along with the provision of basic services and decent transportation systems. It is also vital that future cities improve resource efficiency and resilience to disasters, as well as mitigating and adapting to climate change.

The expansion of wealthier cities, meanwhile, must be carefully managed to optimise their social, economic and cultural potential. The following case studies present innovative and ambitious projects that aim to provide a foundation for a better quality of life and enhanced opportunities for all citizens.

BiodiverCity Penang

BIG +
Hijjas +
Ramboll

In 2020, Bjarke Ingels Group (BIG) won an international competition organised by Penang State Government to design a masterplan for Penang South Islands in Malaysia. Its proposal, called BiodiverCity, responds to the region's cultural diversity and unique ecosystem by providing space for people and nature to coexist. A cluster of artificial islands will accommodate urban districts connected by natural corridors providing habitats for native species. In total, the development will extend over 1,800 hectares and will be home to between 15,000 and 18,000 residents. It will include 4.6 kilometres of public beaches, 240 hectares of parks and a 25-kilometre waterfront.

The masterplan developed by BIG in collaboration with architecture firms Hijjas and Ramboll, is designed as a mixed-use city, with each zone focusing on specific functions. One island will contain governance and research institutions, along with a creative district and an area for conferences and education. A second island will be dedicated to businesses, and a third will contain housing organised around a central marina.

Eight smaller islands will form a miniature archipelago with additional accommodation and straightforward access for fishermen to a network of waterways. Sustainability is a key focus of the project, which will see buildings constructed using low-carbon materials such as bamboo and local timber. Green roofs, facades and parks will contribute to the creation of new habitats, while a water-, air- and land-based transportation network will make roads and cars redundant, creating safer and cleaner neighbourhoods.

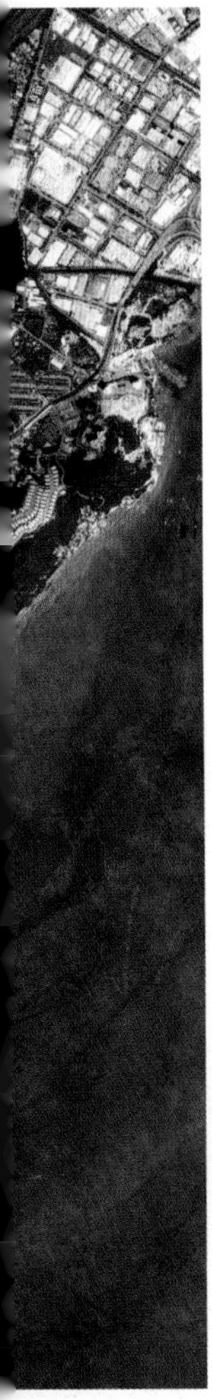

← The masterplan for Penang South Islands focuses on liveability, sustainability and social and economic inclusivity

Autonomous public transportation enables a car-free environment

Three islands form mixed-use districts accommodating 15,000 to 18,000 residents across more than 1,800 hectares

Port of Tallinn

Zaha Hadid Architects

Many existing cities feature districts that require redevelopment to make them suitable for future uses. Zaha Hadid Architects won a competition to revitalise the Old City Harbour in the Estonian capital, Tallinn, which is currently difficult to access and designed only for transit. The city's Masterplan 2030 project aims to improve the fast-growing port's connections with the historic city centre and its public spaces, creating a vibrant new destination containing land for civic use and development.

The design is structured around an urban promenade that forms a landscaped green corridor linking the ferry and cruise terminals to parks and other landmarks. New zones dedicated to culture, entertainment, shopping and hotels will serve Tallinn's residents and the growing number of annual visitors who will arrive into the port. Residential areas built on reclaimed land will provide an attractive alternative to the city's Soviet-era housing blocks, and offices and university buildings will help reinforce its status as a leading hub for technology firms and digital start-ups.

The architectural approach applied across the masterplan seeks to maintain a connection to the city's rich history through the use of appropriate materials, textures and building volumes. New buildings displaying a more contemporary style will also serve to differentiate the port from the rest of the city centre. A landmark tower positioned on a breakwater at the entrance to the port will act as a beacon for the new district, encapsulating its progressive values.

Tallinn's Masterplan 2030 creates a vibrant new district in the existing port area

A landmark tower welcomes millions of visitors arriving by cruise ship each year

↑ New connections will be formed between the port and the historic city centre
← The masterplan consolidates and improves the port's existing functions while offering land for civic use and development

Nanjing Zendai Himalayas Center

MAD Architects

The masterplan for Nanjing Zendai Himalayas Center in Nanjing, China, embodies the Chinese architect Ma Yansong's Shanshui City concept, which seeks to restore spiritual harmony between nature and humanity within the modern urban environment. The design for the 56-hectare development endeavours to balance Nanjing's historic past and its high-tech future, immersing inhabitants in nature while providing all of the conveniences of modern living.

The masterplan developed by Ma's Beijing-based practice MAD Architects features 13 undulating towers that surround a village-like cluster of low-rise buildings nestled into the landscape. The white, curved-glass louvres covering the towers evoke the shapes of nearby mountains and rivers. Ponds, streams and waterfalls connect the buildings with landscaping that includes plenty of trees, plants and green spaces aimed at creating a spiritual retreat in the middle of the city.

Ma has said that applying the *shan shui* philosophy to city-scale projects results in architecture that is more sensitive to the human experience, as well as helping people feel more connected to the environment. The Nanjing masterplan provides a blueprint for future development that is architecturally rich and poetic, while still fulfilling the everyday needs of modern city dwellers.

← The masterplan includes natural spaces for contemplation surrounded by mountain-like towers

Shenzhen Cultural District

MVRDV

Shenzhen was designated a Special Economic Zone by the Chinese government in 1979. Since then it has grown rapidly from a town of 30,000 inhabitants into one of the world's largest and most progressive megacities, with a population exceeding 12 million. The city is a major manufacturing hub and is home to many of China's biggest technology corporations. In the early 2000s the municipal government laid out a strategy to transition the economy towards cultural and creative industries. As part of this project, Dutch firm MVRDV developed a proposal to turn a former industrial area in east Shenzhen into a vibrant cultural hub focused on the arts.

The conceptual masterplan for the Shenzhen Cultural District is based around a mountain-like volume that rises above its surroundings to provide views over a new green park. The park covers the roofs of buildings added along the existing street layout. Gaps between these buildings create a spacious streetscape down below that is shaded from the harsh summer sun. The masterplan incorporates some of the existing warehouses, with new skyscrapers combining to form the 180-metre-high mountain. The speculative proposal, designed for a developer-led creative complex called OCT Loft, demonstrates a vision for the future of Shenzhen that combines its ambitions to become a global centre for cutting-edge culture with a focus on creating high-quality public space.

← Parks cover the roofs of buildings that shade a network of streets incorporating cantilevered arcades

Liuzhou Forest City

Stefano Boeri Architetti

The city of Liuzhou in the southern Chinese province of Guangxi is one of the world's most smog-affected urban areas. Italian firm Stefano Boeri Architetti was commissioned by Liuzhou Municipality Urban Planning to develop a masterplan for a new green city spanning around 175 hectares along the Liu River north of Liuzhou. The design is based on the Vertical Forest concept Boeri originally implemented in Milan, Italy, and will be home to 30,000 inhabitants. They will be joined by approximately 40,000 trees and one million plants, which will help to absorb carbon dioxide and microparticles, as well as producing oxygen to combat the issue of air pollution.

The plants and trees will be situated not just along avenues and in parks and gardens, but also on the facades of buildings. The abundant greenery will help the city merge with the surrounding forests, creating an expanded ecosystem for birds, insects and small animals. The masterplan's layout follows the site's topography, while the undulating shapes of the buildings evoke the silhouette of the nearby mountains. A high-speed railway will connect the city with Liuzhou, and roads will be reserved for electrically powered vehicles. Solar panels and geothermal power will ensure the city is self-sufficient from an energy point of view, making it a pioneering example of China's commitment to cleaner and greener urban development.

The masterplan implements the concept of biodiversity on an urban scale

Oberbillwerder

ADEPT
+ Karres
en Brands

With this competition-winning proposal for a new urban district on the outskirts of Hamburg, Danish architecture office ADEPT and Dutch studio Karres en Brands address several important issues concerning the future expansion of cities into adjacent green belt or agricultural areas. The 124-hectare Oberbillwerder site is located in an interstitial zone between the city and the countryside that currently lacks a cohesive identity or development strategy. The vision for a 'Connected City' with a rapid transit link to central Hamburg will create a vibrant and liveable new district that retains its connection with the natural surroundings.

The existing landscape of rectangular fields separated by dikes informed Oberbillwerder's geometric layout, which comprises distinct neighbourhoods connected by green and blue arteries in the form of parks and waterways. New streets will prioritise pedestrians, cyclists and public transport. An 'anti-iconic' approach to the development's architecture will result in buildings that draw their identity from the surroundings. Residents will be able to choose from various housing typologies designed to facilitate canal-side living, landscape living or urban living.

Nature will be integrated into the masterplan by way of preserved marshlands and rivers, along with a cultivated landscape for farming and an activity landscape dedicated to sports and recreation. The values laid out in the masterplan are intended to guide a process that will see the city evolve in response to the needs of its occupants, while retaining a consistent conceptual vision.

Lively neighbourhoods and amenities are integrated into the cultivated farming landscape

Neighbourhoods organised around small public squares are linked by open green spaces

↖ Green spaces include areas for relaxation as well as communal gardens
↑ Accommodation options include waterfront townhouses, city-centre apartments and detached family homes
← The model district promotes sport, health and activity

Jigna Eco-Community

Skidmore, Owings & Merrill

Like many major metropolises in sub-Saharan Africa, Abuja is experiencing a population boom, with almost nine million people expected to live in the Nigerian capital by 2025. To ease the pressure on Abuja's already overcrowded neighbourhoods, Africa's largest urban land developer, Rendeavour, is constructing a 757-hectare planned community in the hills bordering the city's Outer Northern Expressway (ONEX).

Global architecture and urban planning firm Skidmore, Owings & Merrill (SOM) has designed the concept masterplan for the Jigna Eco-Community, which will form a new sustainable neighbourhood just a short commute from the city centre. The design aims to preserve the site's natural character by nestling into the lush, hilly terrain. A vibrant town centre with views to the north, south and west will be surrounded by a series of residential neighbourhoods that are oriented to optimise their particular location. These communities are laid out to minimise walking distances to local amenities, therefore promoting active lifestyles and reducing vehicle traffic.

SOM worked with Toronto-based Moriyama & Teshima Partners to establish landscape preservation strategies for the ecosystems within and surrounding the site. This ecologically sensitive approach aims to provide a sustainable blueprint for future urban communities in Africa. SOM is applying similar principles to other projects on the continent, including a new Central Business District outside Nairobi, Kenya, a mixed-use model community east of Lagos, Nigeria, and a large development in Ghana's capital, Accra.

← Jigna aims to provide a tranquil urban lifestyle in an ecologically rich setting

↑ Residential communities are designed with local amenities no more than a five-minute walk away

↑ The masterplan takes advantage of the site's natural terrain and preserves its delicate ecosystems

3.

An effective transit system is vital to the success of any major city. The efficient movement of people, goods and supplies saves time and money, helping businesses operate more profitably and making daily life more comfortable and

and

Transportation

convenient for citizens. Due to the complex infrastructure involved, urban mobility is slow to evolve. However, new technologies are prompting a re-evaluation of transportation as cities seek to become cleaner, greener and smarter.

Infrastructure

Research compiled by the World Health Oganization has identified the combustion of fossil fuels by vehicles as one of the main sources of air pollution and greenhouse gas emissions.[1] As a consequence, many countries are set to ban the sale of traditional petrol and diesel cars in the coming decades. Electric vehicles offer a cleaner alternative to fossil fuel-powered transportation that requires minimal adaptation of existing infrastructure. This transition to cleaner energy sources should help reduce smog and improve urban air quality, while the replacement of traditional petrol stations with innovative electric alternatives such as the ones designed by architecture firm Cobe (page 60) could make the refuelling experience more pleasant for drivers.

Advances in driverless automotive technologies also look set to revolutionise mobility within cities. Fleets of shared autonomous vehicles could make car ownership redundant, freeing up space currently used for parking. By moving in closer proximity to each other, driverless vehicles also take up less space on streets. Self-driving service vehicles such as Renault's EZ-PRO concept could replace the ubiquitous courier vans currently clogging up urban road networks, and could also be used as mobile bars, cafés or workshops.

Urban air mobility also looks set to revolutionise how we will move around in future cities. Visions of flying cars that once seemed like science fiction are much closer to becoming reality due to recent advances in materials science, and electric motor and battery technologies. Many leading aerospace companies are working on electric vertical take-off and landing (eVTOL) aircraft, which operate like helicopters and could be used for moving passengers or cargo around or between cities.

---

1 F. Karagulian, C. A. Belis, C. G. Dora, A. M. Prüss-Ustün, S. Bonjour, H. Adair-Rohani et al., 'Contributions to Cities' Ambient Particulate Matter (PM): A Systematic Review of Local Source Contributions at Global Level', *Atmospheric Environment* 120 (2015): 475–83.

Once these aircraft have met the rigorous regulatory requirements for commercial passenger travel, eVTOL firms such as Lilium (page 72) believe they will be able to launch commercial operations as soon as 2024.

While the most advanced plans for eVTOL transportation involve piloted vehicles, unmanned aerial vehicles (UAVs), or drones, are already being trialled to perform deliveries or other tasks within cities. Amazon, Flirtey, Wing (a subsidiary of Alphabet Inc.) and several other firms have developed autonomous drones that could provide cleaner and more efficient alternatives to current land-based last-mile delivery services. Design agency PriestmanGoode's drone delivery concept, Dragonfly (page 80), shows parcels being delivered directly to drop-off points incorporated into the architecture of apartment buildings.

The next step for aerial mobility will involve refining the user experience and exploring how to incorporate the necessary infrastructure into cities. MVRDV's collaboration with Airbus (page 74) and Pickard Chilton's eVTOL hub concept for Uber (page 76) examine how future skyports might integrate with other mobility solutions to enable journeys that are convenient, affordable, connected and personalised.

Another technology set to disrupt the transportation sector is hyperloop – a system comprising pods that move through reduced-pressure tubes at airline speeds. The open-source design was initially released by Tesla and SpaceX, with several companies now working to develop the technologies. If implemented successfully, hyperloop could provide a faster alternative to existing methods of transportation that would reduce the pressure on housing in cities by allowing commuters to live further away.

We can't yet know exactly how driverless cars, drones, eVTOL aircraft or hyperloop might affect the way we move around cities, as most of these technologies require years, or perhaps decades, of further development and testing before they will be ready for use. There is, however, a consensus that mobility must become more efficient and less polluting, so there is unprecedented scope for alternative transportation and infrastructure solutions that meet these next-generation requirements.

New Deal Paris

Carlo Ratti Associati

For an exhibition organised in 2019 by the Forum métropolitain du Grand Paris, architect Carlo Ratti's Milan-based studio proposed a series of alternative futures for Paris's major roads, including the famous Boulevard périphérique. Working as part of a team led by SEURA Architectes, Carlo Ratti Associati was responsible for envisioning what the road system might look like in the year 2050.

The proposals are informed by technological innovations including electric and autonomous vehicles, which facilitate cleaner, quieter, more efficient and connected transportation infrastructure. One of the visions suggests halving the number of car lanes on the Périphérique to free up space for a reconfigurable playground, built using modular paving tiles that could be moved around to provide different functions throughout the day. Another concept called Habiter les Dessus (Living Above) would see green buildings constructed above the Périphérique to connect the historical city inside it with the poorer suburbs outside.

Ratti also developed visions for three suburban highways in the Île-de-France district, including a proposal for reducing the number of car lanes on the mammoth A6 motorway from 12 to 4, creating space along the centre for greenhouses or a photovoltaic plant. The final two ideas focused on using real-time mobility data to create more efficient public transport and improved public space.

← Transforming the Boulevard périphérique into a space for living, playing and farming

Ultra-Fast Charging Station for Electric Cars

Cobe + Clever

Surging sales of electric vehicles (EVs) and plug-in hybrids have led governments and city municipalities to begin developing infrastructure to support the shift to cleaner and greener transportation. Danish architecture firm Cobe and e-mobility provider Clever have developed a modular system for ultra-fast charging stations, which are being rolled out across Europe in an attempt to revolutionise the experience of driving and recharging an EV.

The charging stations are designed to provide drivers with a pleasant environment for relaxing while waiting for their car to charge. The architectural form and use of sustainable materials reflect the green technology of EVs. The clean design and natural aesthetic contrast with the noise and pollution associated with traditional fuel-based petrol stations.

Each charging station uses a modular kit of timber components to create treelike canopies sheltering the vehicles and drivers. The canopies can be combined in numerous configurations depending on the site requirements and can be disassembled for reuse or upcycling of materials. Local trees and plants can be incorporated into the landscaping of the station to increase biodiversity, and the green roofs are fitted with downpipes that channel rainwater to natural seepage areas. The resulting green oasis is intended to create an opportunity for drivers and passengers to unwind in a calm, natural setting.

← Charging stations for electric cars built from a modular kit of timber components

BILVASK
WASH WORLD
WASH WORLD
BLIV I BILEN
STAY IN CAR
STOP
STOP
WASH WORLD
BILVASK
UBEGRÆNSET
69.-
ENKELT
39.-
ÅBEN
7-22

↖ Creating spaces where drivers and passengers can enjoy a meaningful break during their journey

EZ-PRO

Renault

The evolution of autonomous vehicles is set to radically alter how we live in cities. Driverless cars will make citizens less reliant on vehicle ownership, as well as transforming the layout and infrastructure of streets and reducing traffic. These vehicles will also play an important role in the e-commerce revolution, facilitating the last-mile delivery of parcels and services.

Renault's EZ-PRO concept demonstrates how fleets of modular, connected robo-vehicles could be deployed to deliver items directly to a client or to a designated collection point within a city. Customisable pods fitted with secure lockers would collect parcels from distribution centres outside the city. A 'leader pod' staffed by a concierge who oversees deliveries from the vehicle's cockpit would be followed by a convoy of autonomous pods that could travel independently to various drop-off points. The pods could also be adapted to perform various functions within an urban context, such as operating as coffee bars or small workshops.

The EZ-PRO would be integrated into the ecosystem of smart cities, so transport authorities could optimise both the number of vehicles in circulation and their routes to minimise congestion. An all-electric motor would reduce noise and emissions, and the pods would charge through dynamic induction while driving on roads with integrated cabling. Alongside Renault's EZ-GO concept for public transport, the EZ-PRO provides a vision for future mobility that is autonomous, electric, connected and designed to enhance the convenience of urban living.

← EZ-PRO could make last-mile deliveries smarter and more efficient

↑ The autonomous pods could perform numerous roles within the urban environment

EZ-Pro

EZ-Pro

Lilium Vertiports

Aviation company Lilium has developed an all-electric vertical take-off and landing (eVTOL) jet aircraft that could become one of the first to enable high-speed regional transportation for business and leisure customers. One of the key benefits of eVTOL aircraft is that they can connect towns and cities without the cost and complexity of traditional transportation infrastructure. All they require are spaces called vertiports, from which they can take off and land, much like a helicopter.

Lilium's objective is to enable fast and seamless journeys between locations that are integrated into existing urban transportation networks. The company has created a proposal for modular and scalable vertiports that could be placed in convenient locations such as at an existing transportation hub, beside a shopping centre, on top of a car park or alongside a suburban residential development.

Each vertiport includes a landing and take-off area, a parking stand and a terminal. Passengers will arrive at the terminal having prebooked their journey using a dedicated app. They will board and disembark the Lilium jet at the parking stands, where the aircraft will be cleaned, checked and charged. Vertiports will also require air traffic control technology and will need to comply with aviation safety regulations. Lilium has partnered with global infrastructure operator Ferrovial to begin developing a network of vertiports, initially in major cities across the US state of Florida.

← Vertiports located in urban and suburban settings

Airbus UAM

MVRDV + Airbus

As one of the world's leading aviation firms, Airbus is well positioned to set the agenda for the future of urban air mobility (UAM). The company has established a team of designers, urbanists and sociologists to examine how the integration of UAM into existing transportation networks might change the way people move around in cities. Architecture firm MVRDV has consulted on the project, exploring how UAM could help cities evolve and expand in ways that are sustainable and accessible to people from all backgrounds.

The studio looked at how vertiports for take-off and landing could be plugged into a city's existing architecture and infrastructure. It proposed integrating educational and healthcare facilities or business hubs alongside vertiports to help transform underdeveloped neighbourhoods into vibrant networking districts. The firm's research also suggested that vertiports could serve to connect disadvantaged areas of cities and remote places without the need for expensive or disruptive infrastructure.

MVRDV's vision shows vertiports that connect with multimodal last-mile transportation options, including autonomous vehicles, buses, trams and bicycles. Hubs of various types and sizes could form part of a three-dimensional mobility network, connecting places currently fractured by existing infrastructure such as roads and railway tracks. Airbus is also addressing the crucial technical and safety concerns associated with UAM by developing an unmanned traffic management system that would safely coordinate the movement of thousands of autonomous aerial vehicles flying over a city.

↖ Vertiports enhance accessibility between disconnected areas
↑ Take off and landing pads incorporated into multistorey transportation hubs
← Vertiports as part of a green mobility network

Uber Sky Tower

Pickard Chilton + ARUP

In recent years, ridesharing service Uber has worked with leading architects, engineers and aviation experts to explore what the future of its service might look like when urban air mobility becomes logistically and economically feasible. Its aerial ridesharing division Uber Elevate was purchased in 2020 by transportation company Joby Aviation, which is developing an eVTOL passenger aircraft that it intends to operate as early as 2023.

At Uber's Elevate Summit in 2018, US architecture firm Pickard Chilton and engineering specialist ARUP presented a vision for an eVTOL hub that would be capable of handling up to 1,000 take-offs and 1,000 landings per hour. With a footprint of just 1.2 hectares or less, the mega skyport would allow the aircraft to land, dock and recharge on moveable platforms that would transition through the building using a system of elevators to save space and increase throughput. Passengers would board and disembark in dedicated areas separated from active aircraft operations.

The modular tower could be constructed in horizontal or vertical configurations in different urban contexts, such as above a highway or on top of an existing building. It would also connect with other transportation infrastructure such as railways, buses and autonomous vehicles to allow passengers to complete their journey. The Uber Sky Tower presents a radical vision for urban aviation infrastructure that is efficient, scalable and capable of supporting busy, multimodal operations.

← The Sky Tower is a vision for a next-generation urban aviation transport system

↑ The mega-skyport could facilitate 1,000 arrivals and 1,000 departures per hour
↗ The modular construction system could be applied vertically or horizontally to suit different contexts
→ The concept is designed to support Uber's vision for the future of intra-urban transportation

Dragonfly

PriestmanGoode

Drone deliveries are currently being trialled by leading online retailers and delivery firms as a way to relieve congestion in urban areas and fulfil last-mile parcel deliveries. London design studio PriestmanGoode's proposal for an integrated drone delivery system called Dragonfly examines how future cities might adapt to optimise the benefits of these services.

The Dragonfly system uses a city's waterways as the base for autonomous barges that act as mobile distribution points and charging stations. Dragonfly drones would pick up parcels from the boats and deliver them to dedicated docking pads located on the sides of buildings or on their rooftops. In a film produced by PriestmanGoode to illustrate the project, the drones are seen drifting between buildings and depositing parcels with customers on the upper floors of skyscrapers, before returning to the barge.

The system aims to reduce congestion caused by delivery vans and could help to reclaim the streets for people rather than cars. If demand for drone deliveries increases in the coming years and decades, the design of buildings and infrastructure in future cities will need to change to accommodate this alternative form of delivery logistics.

← Dragonfly demonstrates how cities could adapt to future uses of drone technology

Virgin Hyperloop

In 2020, Virgin Hyperloop became the first company to conduct a hyperloop passenger test, sending two of its own executives on a journey through a 500-metre-long vacuum tube in the Nevada desert. Virgin Hyperloop's vision for implementing the system in the future focuses on providing direct and on-demand transportation. Passengers will board a pressurised pod at a nearby hyperloop portal and be transported non-stop to their destination at speeds of over 1,000 kilometres per hour.

Portals will be positioned in urban centres and integrated with other transportation infrastructure to enable seamless, point-to-point travel. It will be possible to configure the portals in different ways to suit their particular context, and low noise levels will enable them to be built closer to city centres. The proposal also suggests that the portals could be incorporated into a landscaped setting to create a versatile and attractive gathering place, or sunk beneath the ground to free up space if required.

The tubes and portals could be covered with solar panels that could generate sufficient renewable energy to power the system. Hyperloop pods could also be used to deliver goods to distribution centres on the outskirts of cities. Virgin Hyperloop is working with partners in the USA, Europe, the Middle East and India on feasibility studies for potential routes and has stated that its goal is to launch commercial operations by 2030.

↖ Passengers board hyperloop pods through airdocks
← Pods travel direct to their destination with no intermediate stops

Hardt Hyperloop Hub

UNStudio

One of the key steps in transforming hyperloop from a revolutionary concept into a practical, affordable and scalable mobility system will be to refine the infrastructure required for it to operate successfully. As part of this ongoing process, hyperloop development firm Hardt worked with Dutch architecture office UNStudio to produce a vision for future European hyperloop stations, and how these might integrate into existing towns and cities.

The Hardt Hyperloop Hub is a modular system for creating stations that are scalable depending on their location. The stations could be positioned in a city centre or a suburb, or integrated into an infrastructure hub such as an airport. The design combines space for platforms and services related to the hyperloop journey with flexible modules that could be used for other activities. For example, UNStudio believes the speed with which hyperloop could deliver fresh food might lead to markets opening next to stations, while new workspaces, meeting places or learning areas could be created within a comfortable commute of existing institutions or offices.

Hubs would generate power using photovoltaic panels set on their roofs. This electricity would power the buildings, as well as autonomous vehicles, buses and bicycles used by passengers to complete their journey. Hardt Hyperloop is currently investigating the feasibility of implementing hyperloop technologies across Europe, including a route between Amsterdam and Frankfurt that would make the 450-kilometre journey possible in around 50 minutes.

← Hyperloop hubs reduce waiting times and facilitate rapid transit between destinations

4.

Urban populations are disproportionately vulnerable to the effects of climate change and air pollution, which are worsening as a consequence of urban-based activities.[1] According to UN-Habitat, cities produce more than 70 per cent of the world's carbon dioxide emissions.[2] In addition, more than 80 per cent of people

1 See S. Revi et al., 'Urban Areas', in *Climate Change 2014: Impacts, Adaptation, and Vulnerability. Part A: Global and Sectoral Aspects. Contribution of Working Group II to the Fifth Assessment Report of the Intergovernmental Panel on Climate Change*, ed. C. B. Field et al. Cambridge and New York: Cambridge University Press, pp. 535–612; available online at www.ipcc.ch/site/assets/uploads/2018/02/WGIIAR5-Chap8_FINAL.pdf

2 UN-Habitat, *Cities and Climate Change: Global Report on Human Settlements*, 2011.

and

Green Architecture

living in urban areas that monitor air pollution are exposed to air quality levels that exceed World Health Organization (WHO) limits.[3] Solutions to these issues need to be identified and implemented quickly in order to protect the health and well-being of current and future generations of urban citizens.

3 World Health Organization, *Ambient Air Pollution: A Global Assessment of Exposure and Burden of Disease*, 2016.

Urban Farms

Scientific studies have shown that one of the best ways to mitigate some of the environmental concerns associated with rapid urbanisation is to include green spaces in cities.[4] Parks, gardens and green roofs can all be used to reduce the heat-island effect caused by heat becoming trapped in built-up areas. Green roofs help to insulate the structures below and regulate rainwater that falls on buildings while also filtering out pollutants. Trees are another useful tool that can be employed to aid the creation of cleaner and greener urban spaces. Not only do they absorb harmful airborne particulates and other pollutants, they can also help mitigate noise pollution and support biodiversity by providing ecosystems that are important for all kinds of insect and bird species.

The psychological impact of our increasing disconnect from nature is another reason why municipalities are looking to increase the amount of green space in cities. Regular interaction with nature can help increase happiness, alleviate stress and boost productivity.[5] Research into the theory known as 'biophilia' suggests that humans respond positively to cues such as vegetation, lakes and waterways. Urban green spaces such as parks, playgrounds and gardens can also reduce morbidity and mortality in urban residents by stimulating social cohesion and supporting physical activity.

The garden city movement pioneered by English urban planner Ebenezer Howard (1850–1928) in the late nineteenth century provided an early blueprint for how to capture the benefits of both urban and countryside living through intelligently planned development. Howard's vision of self-sufficient communities with plenty of space for parks

---

4 A. Tiwari, P. Kumar, G. Kalaiarasan and T.-B. Ottosen, "The Impacts of Existing and Hypothetical Green Infrastructure Scenarios on Urban Heat Island Formation', *Environmental Pollution* 274 (2020): 115898. DOI: 10.1016/j.envpol.2020.115898.

5 C. Sardar, C. Webster and J. Gallacher, 'Residential Greenness and Prevalence of Major Depressive Disorders: A Cross-sectional, Observational, Associational Study of 94,879 Adult UK Biobank Participants', *Lancet Planet Health* 2.4 (2018): e162-e173. DOI: 10.1016/S2542-5196(18)30051-2.

and agriculture was founded on socialist ideals, whereas today a premium is often placed on residential and commercial property with access to good-quality outdoor environments.
Contemporary projects that combine exceptional buildings with communal green spaces, such as the Toronto ORCA scheme designed by Safdie Architects (page 96), can help to improve a city's public realm and are more likely to be both financially and ecologically sustainable.

Another concern relating to the sustainability of future cities is access to affordable, healthy food. Cities can address hunger and malnutrition by making healthy foods affordable, available and attractive for all citizens. Urban expansion is also impacting the availability of land on the outskirts of cities that could be used for farming, leading to the lengthening of supply chains and knock-on effects such as increases in transport-related pollution and waste from packaging. One potential solution is the creation of urban farms that provide fresh produce grown within the city, as envisioned by architecture firm Sasaki in its proposal for space-efficient vertical farms in the Chinese city of Shanghai (page 110). Other studios including Precht (page 114) and Framlab (page 118) have developed modular systems for growing food in cities that seek to involve communities in the urban farming process.

Implementing urban farming practices to combat the problems associated with hunger and food inequality could help to make cities better and healthier places to live in. A general greening of these concrete jungles is also vital to ensure a better quality of life for all citizens, as well as contributing to the battle against potentially catastrophic climate change.

Self Sufficient City

WOHA

The work of Singapore architecture office WOHA consistently addresses issues relating to sustainability and community in urban planning. The firm's approach to tropical architecture utilises biophilic building practices to maximise green coverage in an attempt to combat the urban heat-island effect, while also reintroducing biodiversity and green relief into the city.

This conceptual design for a Self Sufficient City accommodating 210,000 inhabitants in northern Jakarta would retain over half of the existing green landscape and incorporate it into a layered 'eco-town in a forest'. The proposed 730-hectare site is overgrown with secondary rainforest, which would form the basis for parkland traversed by paths and tramlines. This diverse topographic landscape would provide a safe, car-free environment containing waterways, pavilions, event spaces, shops and cafés.

Aerial neighbourhoods comprising 'sky streets' and 'sky parks' built into and on top of residential and workplace buildings would create an inverted skyline with rooftops capped at the same height. A canopy comprising more than three square kilometres of photovoltaic panels would cover the seamless rooftops, and would generate enough electricity to support the fully net-zero-energy city. The panels would also act as a sun shade, protecting 'sky fields' where produce could be grown to feed the city's inhabitants. Ideas contained within this speculative proposal inform many of WOHA's built projects and provide a blueprint for more sustainable and sociable urban development.

← The Garden City concept reimagined as a multilayered, high-density megacity

← Residential and workplace zones are layered above the existing tropical landscape

Pirelli 39 — Diller Scofidio + Renfro + Stefano Boeri Architetti

This project combines two architectural approaches that will be key to the sustainable evolution of major cities: adaptive reuse of existing buildings and the introduction of greenery to the streetscape. The design team of Diller Scofidio + Renfro and Stefano Boeri Architetti won an international competition to revitalise a site in Milan's Porta Nuova Gioia district. The mixed-use development involves the refurbishment of a 28-storey office tower and a 7-storey podium building straddling Via Melchiorre Gioia, along with the construction of an environmentally responsible residential tower.

The bridge building will be converted into a cultural hub containing a new biodiverse greenhouse intended as an extension of the neighbouring Biblioteca degli Alberi park. The centre will provide an immersive educational experience dedicated to teaching visitors about plants. Using principles previously applied by Stefano Boeri at the nearby Bosco Verticale towers, the new residential building will feature 1,700 square metres of vegetation distributed across its floors. The architects claim the plants will absorb the equivalent amount of carbon dioxide and produce the same amount of oxygen per year as a 10,000-square-metre forest. The project's focus on the adaptive reuse of the existing buildings rather than demolition and reconstruction reinforces its sustainable credentials, while the abundant planting will help to improve air quality in a busy part of the city.

↖ The new tower's vegetation will absorb 14 tonnes of CO_2 and produce 9 tonnes of oxygen per year
← A biodiverse greenhouse space will provide an immersive educational experience

Toronto ORCA

Safdie Architects

Toronto ORCA aims to transform the site of an active rail corridor in downtown Toronto into a 6.5-hectare mixed-use urban development centred around a 4.5-hectare publicly accessible park. The proposal involves constructing a deck across the 100-metre-wide rail corridor to create a vibrant green space in the heart of the site.

Vehicular access and parking are situated within the decking structure to make the park a safe space for pedestrians and cyclists. Landscaping and paths reinforce connections with the existing network of streets and green areas, while retail units, restaurants and cafés on multiple levels open directly onto the park. Planting is incorporated into stepped balconies that articulate the facades of the residential buildings, and residents have access to roof gardens on top of elevated bridges linking the towers.

Toronto ORCA is the latest evolution of Safdie Architects' concept of the three-dimensional city, explored in projects like Habitat 67, Marina Bay Sands, Sky Habitat and Raffles City Chongqing. The horizontal and vertical interconnectivity of nature and the built environment in these projects helps to humanise the urban realm. In contrast to the introverted, solitary high-rise, the clustering of towers connected with the park emphasises collective amenities, connection to nature and community engagement.

← The ORCA project features a large park created above a major rail corridor

Vehicular access and parking are incorporated within the decking structure to maximise the amount of publicly accessible open space

1Hotel Paris

Kengo Kuma & Associates

Japanese architect Kengo Kuma describes his design for the 1Hotel in Paris as a 'green lung for the city'. The hotel will be located on the left bank of the River Seine and will serve as a landmark for the Paris Rive Gauche neighbourhood. Plants will cover the building's facades and roof terraces, creating a natural counterpoint to the dense urban context of the avenue de France. The building's elevations are broken up into a series of triangular wooden volumes that form balconies and terraces – many of which will be used as planters. This sculptural, fragmented facade structure will help to reduce the building's visual mass and create the appearance of a naturally eroded surface.

A lush public garden will be positioned between the U-shaped 1Hotel and a separate volume containing a youth hostel designed by Paris studio Marchi Architects. The garden will provide a retreat from the city and will be linked to a green space on the avenue de France by a passageway lined with double-height wooden pillars.

Kengo Kuma is known for using materials such as wood and stone to create buildings that achieve harmony with nature. He believes that the scale of architecture and the choice of materials can help make future cities more sustainable and pleasant to live in. The 1Hotel Paris project encapsulates these ideas in its modular timber construction and use of abundant greenery, presenting a vision for urban architecture that appears to be shaped by nature.

← The building is designed to look as if it was shaped by a process of natural erosion

← Terraces and suspended gardens are visible from inside and outside the hotel
↑ The design combines warm wood with reflective metal panels

A public garden will provide a space for contemplation within the dense urban context

Southbank by Beulah

UNStudio
+ Cox Architecture

UNStudio and Cox Architecture won an international competition to design this pair of plant-covered skyscrapers in Melbourne's Southbank area. Upon completion, the larger tower will be the world's tallest vertical garden, at a height of 365 metres. The project is organised around a 'Green Spine' that aims to extend the verdant public realm from the nearby Botanical Gardens and Southbank Boulevard. The twisting forms of the high-rise structures encompass a network of landscaped platforms, terraces and verandahs, covering a total area in excess of 12,500 square metres.

The mixed-use building will host commercial spaces alongside residential units and a hotel. The Green Spine is designed to encourage the flow of movement from the boulevard into the building. It extends upwards from the public park on top of the podium to connect with various amenities as it rises and twists, culminating in a garden at the top of the residential tower. The lower- and mid-storey levels feature smaller-scale shrub planting, while taller plants and trees are incorporated into winter gardens on the upper storeys. The planting is intended to absorb noise and air pollution, with carefully positioned trees and ferns helping to shade the interiors from harsh summer sunlight.

Pocket parks, terraces and verandahs form a 'Green Spine' that rises between two twisting towers

↑ The podium incorporates a public park on its upper level
→ Green spaces extend upwards to a sky garden at the top of the residential tower

Sunqiao Urban Agricultural District

Sasaki

As the world's largest agricultural producer and consumer, China must adapt its farming practices in the coming decades to compensate for a rapid loss of farmland to urbanisation. One possible solution is to create vertical farms on the outskirts of cities that could supply the population with locally grown produce. A proposal by US-based design firm Sasaki for a new farming district in the Shanghai suburb of Sunqiao demonstrates how cities could use vertical farming to improve the management of agricultural resources in the future.

The Sunqiao Urban Agricultural District would comprise buildings filled with hydroponic and aquaponic systems for growing vegetables including leafy greens like kale, spinach and pak choi. Stacking the growing beds vertically reduces the amount of space required in a region where land is very expensive. The vertical food factories would form part of a new district focused on agricultural innovation, research and experiences that would inform citizens about urban food production. Laboratories, offices and exhibition spaces would be surrounded by public spaces showcasing various aspects of urban farming in action, including outdoor planters, vines and interactive greenhouses. By educating future generations about where their food comes from, the project aims to promote a more sustainable way of living in China's expanding cities.

← Greenhouses functioning as vertical food factories educate children about where their food comes from

Sunqiao focuses on weaving agriculture into residential and commercial life

The Farmhouse — Precht

The Farmhouse is a proposal to unite the fundamental human needs of food and shelter in a new form of urban architecture. According to the Food and Agriculture Organization of the United Nations (FAO), 80 per cent of all food produced globally is consumed in urban areas[1] and the predicted global population in 2050 will require food production to rise by around 70 per cent.[2]

In response to these challenges, Austria-based architect Chris Precht has developed a modular building system for creating dwellings that facilitate urban farming. Using these buildings to grow crops would offer an ecological alternative to current food supply systems and provide food security for the city's inhabitants.

The Farmhouse system would consist of prefabricated cross-laminated timber components that are straightforward to transport and install. Apartments based on traditional A-frame houses would contain gardening elements built into an outer layer, with hydroponics and solar power systems used to sustain the plants. The kits could be used to create small units for single-family use, with homeowners able to choose the layout, structure and gardening elements from a catalogue. Taller duplex units could combine to form residential clusters with spaces for gardening in the V-shaped voids between their angled walls. The units could also stack to form towers with a diagrid framework that would optimise the building's footprint. The Farmhouse would allow people living in cities to reconnect with nature and appreciate how food is produced, as well as reducing the need to convert natural environments into farmland.

1 fao.org/urban-food-agenda/en/
2 fao.org/fileadmin/templates/wsfs/docs/Issues_papers/HLEF2050_Global_Agriculture.pdf

← The Farmhouse incorporates infrastructure for urban farming

↑ Food grown on site could be sold to the local community
← The modular building system is inspired by traditional A-frame houses

Glasir

Framlab

Norwegian architect and design engineer Andreas Tjeldflaat developed Glasir as a possible alternative to the damaging practices associated with industrial agriculture. Glasir is a community-based system for urban farming that could provide neighbourhoods with affordable, locally grown produce all year round. The vertical farming structures comprise modules containing aeroponic growing systems that irrigate greens and vegetables using a nutrient-rich mist. The Glasir system consists of five growth modules, three production modules and two access modules, which could be assembled in numerous configurations to form treelike structures. The system's minimal footprint means it could be installed in a backyard or public park or on a pavement – providing a distinctive presence in the streetscape.

Glasir would use sensor-based artificial intelligence software to assess environmental conditions and adapt the composition of modules to suit the local context. Drones could be used to relocate modules within a tree, move them to another tree, return them to their owner or transport them to a service facility. Tjeldflaat designed Glasir to support the provision of affordable and nutritious food in areas of Brooklyn with the highest rates of food insecurity. He believes the system could help improve users' awareness of hyperlocal food supply and the importance of a healthy diet, with each structure providing a symbol of fellowship and resilience for the local community it serves.

← Glasir's aeroponic greenhouse modules combine to form a treelike structure

5.

Throughout history people have chosen to live in cities so they can collaborate and optimise opportunities for sharing knowledge, resources and networks. Digital technologies have made it easier than ever to communicate and share information with other people and with organisations that manage the services and products we interact with every day. The clouds of data

Smart

that constantly surround us all are more dense in cities than anywhere else on the planet, due to the concentration of people in urban areas. As a consequence, cities have become hubs for experimentation and innovation around how these data can be used to make everyday life more efficient, sustainable and affordable.

Cities

So-called 'smart cities' integrate information and communication technologies (ICT) along with physical devices connected to the Internet of Things (IoT) to optimise a city's operations and connect citizens with government. They use sensors and other electronic methods to collect data from people and the urban environment, which are then analysed to facilitate the efficient management of assets, resources and services. The use of data in this way can support and enhance the performance of transport systems, power distribution, crime detection and even rubbish collection. Smart infrastructure can also reduce costs and resource consumption by learning from patterns and adapting in real time, as well as anticipating new needs before they even arise.

Several of the projects presented in this section are described as 'living laboratories' that aim to develop and test new technologies using data gathered from residents and businesses. In this scenario, citizens agree to hand over some personal data in the anticipation that it will be used to improve services for them and their community. Benefits might include access to smart technologies, smart governance, a smart environment, smart mobility and a smart economy. However, there are ethical concerns related to living or working in a smart city, such as the threat of mass surveillance, the governance and ownership of personal data, and issues arising from technocratic inequality within societies.

In many cases, smart cities emerge in areas seeking to stimulate new business, especially in the technology sector. New smart cities or districts often include innovation hubs offering workplaces to companies or entrepreneurs that benefit from having access to assets such as urban data and advanced ICT infrastructure. By marketing their smart credentials, these cities aim to attract the brightest talents to work on producing ground-breaking innovations.

Smart technologies have matured sufficiently for most governments and developers to view them as crucial to the evolution of future cities. Retrofitting this infrastructure into the urban environment is costly and complex, but the process is already well under way in major cities such as Singapore, Dubai and Barcelona. The transformation of Berlin-Tegel Airport into a research and industrial park for innovative urban technologies (page 150) provides an opportunity to combine twentieth-century architecture with twenty-first-century technologies, while the redevelopment of Milan's Expo site into a smart neighbourhood (page 146) will make use of digital infrastructure already installed for the World Fair.

Smart technologies will play an increasingly significant role in the design of new urban developments, as residents come to expect the convenience and enhanced connectivity smart cities provide. The case studies presented over the following pages offer an insight into how these technologies are already an important driver of innovative and ambitious urban planning proposals. Toyota's Woven City project, for example, incorporates autonomous transportation solutions and in-house robotics (page 128), while cryptocurrency firm Blockchains LLC is planning an enormous high-tech community with digital services integrated into its architecture (page 136).

As the roll-out of smart technologies gathers pace over the coming years and decades, it is likely that most of the world's population will soon live in communities that have either been adapted or newly developed to incorporate the latest smart infrastructure. The key to the success of these networked communities will be how seamlessly they blend physical and digital infrastructures in order to make urban areas better places to live in, and how well they protect personal data to ensure it is used only for the benefit of citizens.

BIOTIC

Carlo Ratti Associati

Carlo Ratti Associati describes its masterplan for an extension of Brazil's capital city, Brasília, as 'a high-tech innovation district immersed in nature'. Developed together with consultancy firm EY for real-estate company TerraCap, BIOTIC is a proposal for a 100-hectare development situated between the Brasília National Park and the modernist planned city laid out in 1956 by Lúcio Costa, Oscar Niemeyer and Joaquim Cardozo.

The BIOTIC district is designed as a more human-centred and ecologically sustainable take on Brasília's historic masterplan. The proposal builds on the 'superquadra' concept developed by Costa, which comprised large urban blocks arranged on either side of a highway axis and surrounded by bands of greenery. CRA's plan subdivides these enormous modules into pedestrian-friendly blocks enclosing internal neighbourhoods protected from traffic and pollution.

BIOTIC's citizens will benefit from enhanced contact with nature and spaces that make the most of Brasília's mild climate. Al fresco restaurants and cafés will provide places for smart working, with greenery distributed throughout various plazas, pedestrianised areas, shared allotments, laboratories and retail zones. Office buildings will feature curtain walls that will open up to the outdoors, and digital technologies will be used to manage the effects of sunlight, wind and temperature on the internal climate. Residences, workplaces, plazas and parks are all designed to form a hybrid environment that promotes both social and environmental sustainability.

← Outdoor smart working allows office workers to enjoy Brasília's year-round mild climate

A hybrid environment that promotes both social and environmental sustainability

Woven City — Toyota + BIG

Japanese car giant Toyota has begun constructing a prototype city of the future on a 70-hectare site at the base of Mount Fuji. Woven City is envisioned as a living laboratory where researchers will test and develop technologies such as autonomy, robotics, personal mobility, smart homes and artificial intelligence in a real-world context.

Toyota Motor Corporation worked with BIG on the design of the smart city, which will use data and sensors to connect people, buildings and vehicles via a digital operating system. A virtual version of the city, known as a 'digital twin', is being developed to enable the Woven City team to test connected technologies and the city's software platform while the physical architecture and infrastructure are being constructed.

The city is designed as a network of streets that support different speeds of mobility. Toyota's autonomous e-Palettes will be used for shared transportation and deliveries. A promenade with a mix of lower speed, personal mobility and pedestrians will provide a safe zone, while a park-like promenade will form a green public space containing pedestrianised paths. The three street types will weave together to form city blocks framing parks or courtyards.

Buildings made from sustainable timber and topped with solar panels will be constructed using robotic fabrication techniques. Technologies including in-home robotics and sensor-based artificial intelligence will be used to make everyday life more comfortable, performing functions such as automatic grocery deliveries, laundry collection and waste disposal.

← Toyota is building a prototype city of the future in the foothills of Mount Fuji

Woven City will bring new technologies to life in a real-world environment

↑ Robotic construction will be used to erect timber buildings for housing, retail and business use
→ The city will trial technologies such as in-home robotics and sensor-based artificial intelligence

カフェ
ラウンジ

Smart Forest City Cancun

Stefano Boeri Architetti

Stefano Boeri Architetti developed this masterplan for a sustainable smart city on Mexico's Yucatán Peninsula, which would be driven by values of technological innovation and environmental quality. The metropolitan area near Cancun would cover 550 hectares and host up to 130,000 inhabitants, along with a high-tech innovation campus and research centre aimed at tackling issues related to climate change and creating a more sustainable future for the planet.

The Forest City would incorporate 362 hectares of planted surfaces spread across various parks, roof gardens and green facades. These would be sustainably irrigated using sea water that would be treated at a desalination facility at the city's entrance and distributed via a network of navigable canals. A photovoltaic ring encircling the built area would provide most of the city's energy. Solar panels positioned on raised canopies would also collect rainwater and shelter areas for food cultivation underneath.

Stefano Boeri Architetti worked with engineering and logistics specialist Transsolar to identify smart solutions for optimising the region's natural resources and climate to make the city as self-sufficient as possible. Sensors integrated within buildings would collect data that would be used to support energy management and provide inhabitants with advice on how to save energy and money. Residents would also have access to an app that would map the expected comfort of outdoor spaces, suggesting options for sunny or shaded spots at different times of day.

↖ Smart technologies and mobility solutions reduce the city's energy demands and waste production
← An urban ecosystem in which nature and the city coexist

Blockchains City

Tom Wiscombe Architecture + EYRC

In 2018, software and cryptocurrency firm Blockchains LLC acquired more than 27,000 hectares of land in northern Nevada with the objective of creating a high-tech community based on blockchain technology. Blockchains' objective is to find new ways of interweaving digital identities, digital assets, connected devices and digital payments into everyday life. The organisation describes its vision for a new smart city in the desert as a 'real-life sandbox' that will offer opportunities to experiment with blockchain applications in a real-world context.

The purpose-built urban development will include a residential community, a commercial centre, and a research and development park hosting innovation-led enterprises. Rather than trying to insert smart technologies into an existing context, Blockchains aims to integrate digital services into the city's architecture, infrastructure and governance models. Digital identities based on shared data will enable residents and businesses to interact in new ways with governmental and financial institutions, as well as providers of healthcare, utilities and transportation.

The design for the masterplan developed by Tom Wiscombe Architecture and EYRC Architects includes vast structures called 'mega-mats' that function as cities within a building. Autonomous vehicles will connect different zones within these manufacturing and creative hubs, which also feature civic-scale interior plazas designed as spaces for collaboration. The plans for Blockchains City are anticipated to take several decades to realise, but the impact of blockchain technology on urban living could begin to take effect much sooner.

↖ Blockchain technology would be used to manage the self-governing city's services and cryptocurrency
← Enormous buildings incorporate courtyards that create their own microclimates

Brainport Smart District

UNStudio

Brainport Smart District is a self-learning urban development planned for a 60-hectare site in the Dutch city of Helmond. Designed by Amsterdam-based architecture office UNStudio, the new district will see 1,500 homes and 12 hectares of business premises built over the next ten years, based around a flexible grid layout rather than a predetermined masterplan.

The neighbourhood is described as a 'living lab' that will be used to develop and test new products, services and systems, with residents encouraged to adopt communal resource schemes such as shared energy generation and land cultivation. Data gathered from homes, workplaces and public spaces will feed into a central urban data platform, and will be used by companies to help create new technological solutions focused on improving everyday life for the residents.

All of the infrastructure required to enable data flows is incorporated into the urban development plan, which will evolve to meet the changing needs of the district's inhabitants. There will be a particular focus on new insights and technologies relating to transport, health, energy generation and storage. The development will comprise a mixed residential neighbourhood organised around a central park and surrounded by commercial spaces and nature reserves. The combination of developed zones and natural areas will enable activities related to working, living and leisure to take place side by side. The overall objective is to create a new neighbourhood that does not burden, pollute or exhaust our planet further.

← Smart technologies will enable residents to participate in socio-economic experiments

Residents play an important role in the development of their own living environment

Konza Technopolis

SHoP Architects

As part of Kenya's Vision 2030 economic development programme, the country's Ministry of Information, Communications and Technology is overseeing the creation of Konza Technopolis – a smart city and innovation hub south of Nairobi. SHoP Architects won a competition to develop the masterplan for Konza Technopolis, which hopes to have 200,000 residents by the end of 2030. The masterplan features several linear districts dedicated to specific programmes such as education, residential accommodation, offices, and science and technology. These intersect with mixed-use bands that run in a perpendicular orientation to form a 'stitched' framework, with high-density neighbourhoods at key junctions.

A 60-metre-wide parkscape and public transit corridor extending through the city forms a green boulevard connected to several other parks. Data gathered from smart devices and sensors embedded in roads, buildings and other areas within the urban environment will be shared via a smart communications system and analysed by software to deliver enhanced services to Konza's population. Inhabitants will be able to access the collected data, including traffic maps and detailed descriptions of energy and water consumption, which will help to develop more sustainable living practices and to influence how the city operates. Konza's smart city framework will also be used to optimise services so they meet the needs of residents, workers and visitors.

← Konza is a flagship project of Kenya's Vision 2030 economic development programme

↑ The city is divided into clusters dedicated to housing and various commercial activities
← Smart city infrastructure will support Konza's ICT sector

Milan Innovation District

Carlo Ratti Associati

World Expos aim to showcase innovations and ideas that will shape the future of nations and the world in the coming decades. Following the conclusion of these enormous international exhibitions, Expo sites are often transformed into parks or new urban districts that retain some of the event's pavilions or landmark structures.

In 2017, Carlo Ratti Associati and real estate group Lendlease won a competition to redevelop the 100-hectare site of the Milan World Expo 2015 into a mixed-use neighbourhood dedicated to science, knowledge and technology. The design for the Milan Innovation District (MIND) focuses on setting new standards for urban transformation. Private buildings and public realm will be used to support experiments trialling new ways of working, living and moving around in an urban context. Across the entire site, two storeys at ground level are dedicated as common areas to encourage the sharing of ideas, while an open-source approach to architecture will allow buildings to adapt over time to their users' changing needs.

The site's main thoroughfare – a 1.6-kilometre-long road recalling the *decumanus* that formed the main axis of many Roman cities – will be transformed into a linear park acting as the neighbourhood's core social space. Starting from this axis, the district's streets will become available exclusively for self-driving vehicles. This will help to promote a shared approach to transportation, reducing the volume of traffic and improving the environmental quality. This progressive approach to urban mobility epitomises how MIND will transform the former Expo site into a 'living laboratory' for exploring actions that contribute to a more sustainable future.

← Ground-floor communal spaces create a mixed-use precinct that encourages interaction

↖ The Decumanus forms one of Europe's longest linear parks
↑ The site builds on the Expo's legacy as a place for experimenting with new ways of living

Berlin TXL Urban Tech Republic

Tegel Projekt GmbH + von Gerkan, Marg and Partners Architects

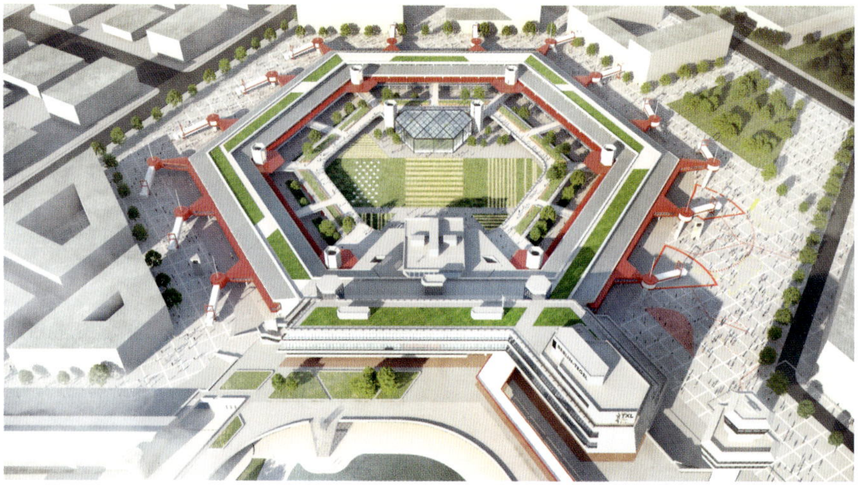

Following the decommissioning of Berlin's Tegel Airport, a decision was made to transform the 500-hectare site into a research and industrial park for innovative urban technologies. von Gerkan, Marg and Partners Architects, the firm behind the design of the original airport, is part of a team involved in redeveloping the site, which includes several buildings that are now listed as historic monuments.

The former airport's entrance building will be transformed into a start-up and innovation centre containing events and conference areas, showrooms, workshops and studios. The outer hexagonal ring that previously housed the jet bridges will be used to accommodate facilities for the Beuth University of Applied Sciences.

In total, the Urban Tech Republic will host up to 1,000 businesses, with the adjacent Kurt-Schumacher-Quartier providing 5,000 residential units and associated amenities. New technologies will be implemented and tested in the Urban Tech Republic, with a focus on mobility, energy and the district's green spaces.

A centre of expertise for urban data called the FUTR HUB will help to develop an infrastructure platform for utilising the future smart city's data. The platform will collect, link and present data gathered from sources including sensors in building ventilation systems, traffic lights and charging stations. The data will be used to enhance the efficiency of technical infrastructure across the site and will feed into projects aimed at creating data-driven solutions and applications for the Internet of Things.

← The former Tegel Airport will become an industrial and research park for urban technologies

↑ The FUTR HUB will research, develop, test and export new technologies
→ Urban data relating to energy, mobility and smart nature will be used to improve services

BAR

Quayside

Sidewalk Labs
+ Waterfront Toronto

Sidewalk Labs was set up by tech giant Alphabet to explore how technological innovation can be used to confront the issues facing contemporary cities. An ambitious proposal for a smart, affordable and climate-positive neighbourhood to be built by Sidewalk Labs on Toronto's eastern waterfront was officially halted in 2020, but many of the ideas featured in the project will continue to be explored in future urban developments.

The Quayside district was set to pioneer the use of open digital infrastructure to provide a shared foundation for urban innovation. Fast, secure and low-cost internet installed throughout households, businesses and the public realm would have enabled constant connectivity for the district's inhabitants. This ubiquitous internet network would have made it more straightforward to gather data for use by researchers, companies and the community to create new services or improve existing ones.

An independent Urban Data Trust was to be established to ensure data gathered in the public realm and some private buildings would be used only for beneficial purposes. These principles of openly sharing data to support urban innovation while enhancing privacy standards will be key to the success of future smart cities. The new district was designed to be built using modular, prefabricated timber components, which could be combined to form different types of buildings. Sidewalk Labs is continuing to develop this standardised, ecologically friendly construction technique for use in future projects.

← A smart district connected by an open digital ecosystem

6.

Major towns and cities already occupy many of the most desirable locations in the world's temperate regions, close to water sources and at points strategically located for trade and tourism. Following decades or centuries of expansion, a significant number

New

of these settlements have now reached the threshold of land suitable for building on, or they soon will. This shortage of space raises the issue of how these cities will deal with any future population increase.

Habitats

An even more grave but not unthinkable concern is what might happen if the Earth itself becomes uninhabitable due to a catastrophe caused by human activity. Where might we go if extreme climate change, biological warfare or a nuclear apocalypse necessitates an evacuation of our home planet? These questions are prompting architects, scientists and intergovernmental organisations to radically rethink how cities might be located and constructed in the future.

This section focuses predominantly on speculative proposals for alternative human habitation. Whether they are designed to address issues occurring now or in the coming decades, these radical solutions are all based on technologies that are currently under development and could influence how cities are planned to support future generations.

One way of confronting the lack of space for urban expansion is to build on water, which covers about 71 per cent of the Earth's surface. Reclaiming land by depositing sand or rubble into shallow water is a well-established technique for creating habitable land from oceans, seas, riverbeds or lake beds. Projects such as Waugh Thistleton's proposal for an inner-city neighbourhood built on a lake in Bergen (page 166) and 10 Design's concept for a new waterfront district in Hong Kong (page 170) show how this process, if managed carefully and creatively, could support sustainable urban expansion.

A more extreme solution for building on water is to design floating buildings, or even entire floating cities. Waterborne communities already exist in various settings around the world, such as the Uru tribe's floating islands in Lake Titicaca, Peru, and the floating communities on the Netherlands' waterways, including Amsterdam's Schoonschip neighbourhood. A 2019 UN-Habitat discussion on floating cities examined their viability as a solution to climate change and a lack of affordable housing. One of the featured proposals called Oceanix City is a floating community for 10,000 people designed to exist in harmony with the ocean (page 160). Another floating city concept developed by SHIMIZU CORPORATION would see a multipurpose tower built within a giant orb submerged in the deep sea (page 164). Both proposals seek to harness the ocean's many resources without damaging marine ecosystems.

Another habitat that could provide an opportunity for future development is the world's deserts. People have inhabited these dry and barren regions for millennia, building some of the world's great cities including Cairo, Riyadh, Lima and Las Vegas. Advances in technologies for passive cooling, solar energy and irrigation could enable large-scale desert communities to be built and sustained more efficiently. One example of how these technologies could be applied is the radical proposal for a vertical city in the Sahara Desert by OXO Architectes (page 176).

The final frontier for human habitation could be the colonisation of other planets – and it might not be as far off as we had previously thought. National and international space agencies, as well as various commercial organisations, have already begun exploring the possibility of colonising the Moon and Mars, and have invited architects to develop visions for habitable buildings and communities. It is likely to be some time before any of these concepts are realised, but in the meantime many of the ideas being proposed could be applied here on Earth. For example, technologies for 3D printing structures from locally available materials and methods for creating a liveable climate in extreme environments could enable self-sufficient communities to be constructed and maintained in new habitats using minimal resources.

Oceanix City

OCEANIX + BIG + Studio Other Spaces + UN-Habitat

Oceanix City is a proposal for a floating community housing 10,000 people, created in response to the imminent threat posed by rising sea levels. OCEANIX, a blue tech company, collaborated with BIG, artist Olafur Eliasson and architect Sebastian Behmann of Studio Other Spaces, UN-Habitat and a team of partners to develop the masterplan for a sustainable floating city that uses blue technologies to meet humanity's shelter, energy, water and food needs while regenerating marine ecosystems.

The city would consist of modular, self-sustaining neighbourhoods covering approximately two hectares each and housing 300 residents. The neighbourhoods would include mixed-use space for living, working and gathering, built around a central area for communal farming. Buildings would be capped at seven storeys to ensure a low centre of gravity and to reduce wind exposure. Clustering neighbourhoods around a protected central harbour would allow larger villages of 12 hectares to accommodate up to 1,650 residents. Social, recreational and commercial functions would be arranged around the inner ring to make it straightforward for residents to navigate the city on foot or using electrically powered boats.

Buildings would be prefabricated on shore using locally sourced materials and towed to the final site to reduce construction costs. The result would be an affordable housing solution that minimises ongoing disruption to Earth's fragile coastal regions.

← A vision for the world's first resilient and sustainable floating community

← Modular neighbourhoods arranged around areas for communal farming
↑ The central harbour incorporates a public square and marketplace

Ocean Spiral

SHIMIZU CORPORATION

A city built underwater might sound like something out of a Jules Verne novel, but there are potential advantages to inhabiting the deep sea. Japanese construction and design firm SHIMIZU CORPORATION has developed a proposal for an undersea structure that extends from the ocean's surface to the seabed, providing a safe, comfortable and healthy environment beneath the waves.

Ocean Spiral comprises a 500-metre-diameter orb connected to the sea floor several kilometres below by a mooring structure and infrastructure spiral. The giant floating globe would contain a city that is less affected by typhoons or earthquakes and exposed to minimal temperature changes due to being largely submerged in the ocean.

A tower within the concrete-framed orb would accommodate the city's inhabitants, who would be employed in the fields of deep-sea energy, research or tourism. Electricity would be generated using ocean thermal energy conversion and sea water would be desalinated using water pressure to provide fresh water. Food would come from a combination of fish farms and plants cultivated using sea water. The Infra Spiral would provide a transportation link to a submarine base and deep-sea monitoring site on the ocean floor.

The project was developed by SHIMIZU CORPORATION's Emerging Frontiers Division, which is dedicated to identifying next-generation technologies and potential new frontiers for human habitation. Ideas and engineering solutions explored in the Ocean Spiral concept could be applied commercially to floating buildings and energy-related infrastructure currently in development.

↖ Ocean Spiral makes the most of the abundant resources, food and energy found in the deep sea

Trenezia

Waugh Thistleton Architects

Lakes, oceans and rivers can be viewed as barriers preventing further urban development, but in some cases water within or near to a city can provide an opportunity. Waugh Thistleton Architects has proposed building a zero-carbon community in the Store Lungegårdsvann Lake, which separates the city centre of Bergen in Norway from its southern districts.

The Trenezia masterplan is a response to the social and economic problems associated with people abandoning the city centre in favour of the suburbs. The new cultural and residential centre would be constructed on the lake and would connect existing neighbourhoods on either side of the water via a new boardwalk. The boardwalk would join up with a walking route around the lake's shore and would accommodate community spaces including a swimming pool, sailing club, performance spaces, cafés and shops. A residential area positioned behind the boardwalk would provide diverse housing options aimed at creating a new, intergenerational community.

Buildings would be graded in height and oriented to ensure even the lowest structures receive plenty of sunlight. The masterplan is driven by environmental factors, utilising advanced timber construction and minimising carbon dioxide emissions across the lifetime of the project. The objective is to demonstrate an innovative solution to the problem of land scarcity in urban centres, and to further Bergen's reputation as a world-leading sustainable city.

← The district connects port areas on opposite shores of the lake

← Streets are oriented to optimise sunlight
↑ Canals include moorings for residents

Redefining Hong Kong's Waterfront

10 Design

Since the late nineteenth century, Hong Kong's developed area has been gradually expanded through extensive land reclamation, enabling exponential population and economic growth. Global architecture firm 10 Design has proposed a visionary concept that addresses masterplanning, resilience and urban issues associated with the city's future development. The project aims to demonstrate how a new neighbourhood built on reclaimed land with improved urban connections could create a more attractive waterfront for residents and tourists. It also explores innovative ecological strategies and ways to introduce new forms of urban agriculture.

The proposal features zones dedicated to commercial, social, civic and ecological activities along the reclaimed waterfront. Pathways linking the metro stations with ferry piers would improve the flow of movement between different destinations. A Vertical Farm Centre housed in a 420-metre tower would provide agricultural services linked to an interactive museum. The tower would also contain a hydroponic greenhouse and a luxury hotel with an aeroponic atrium used to produce crops.

Future implications of climate change would be addressed through resilient architecture that mitigates the effects of typhoons and flash floods. The proposal also includes an aquaculture landscape consisting of interlinked wetlands and low-density fish ponds supported by an artificial reef. The system would help to renew the surrounding marine habitat while filtering sea water to create a clean swimming area linked to a manmade urban beach.

← Reclaimed land accommodates new areas designed to resist flooding and promote urban agriculture

↑ New zones for culture and commerce include a floating market
↗ The Culture Centre and landscaping are designed to combat typhoons and flash floods

Winds blow through the building and retention pods store and purify storm water

City Sand — OXO Architectes

Deserts are among the most inhospitable habitats on Earth, but the consequences of disastrous climate change may make it necessary to one day consider inhabiting such extreme environments. French studio OXO Architectes created the City Sand concept to envision what a futuristic city in the Sahara Desert might look like. The proposal combines all of the city's functions in a towering skyscraper with a vertical garden at its centre. Around the base of the tower, a network of streets set among the dunes would include communal areas such as markets recalling Arabic souks. The building's upper floors would contain residential units, hotels, shops, a panoramic restaurant and a meteorological observatory. Each of the floors would look out across the expanse of the desert, as well as inwards to the garden.

The city is designed to exist autonomously and to be energy self-sufficient. Solar, wind and geothermal energy would all be harnessed to meet the population's energy requirements. The extreme temperature differential between day and night would be used to cool the city overnight. The building's ochre-coloured facades and faceted, rock-like form are intended to help it blend in with the desert. The outer surfaces would incorporate sensor-operated solar shades used to maintain a comfortable internal climate. A huge atrium would contain an inner tower covered with plants. Evaporation and transpiration from the plants and soil would help to create an internal ecosystem suitable for growing the crops required to sustain the city's population.

← The tower rises high above the Sahara Desert
↖ The vertical city contains spaces for living, working and leisure

Project Olympus

ICON + BIG + SEArch+

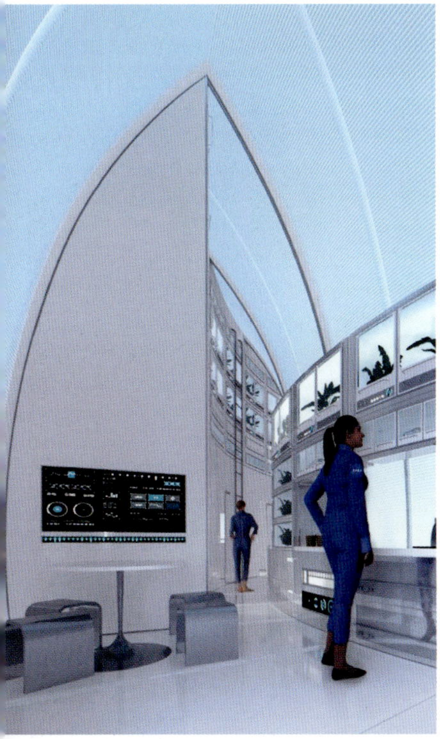

Colonising the Moon or other planets presents many challenges, not least of which is the availability of suitable building materials. Construction technology specialist ICON is working on a possible solution, developing a 3D-printing system that could print structures on the Moon using lunar soil. The US-based company was awarded funding from the National Aeronautics and Space Administration (NASA) to advance the development of additive construction technologies that could be used to create habitats with the required levels of thermal, radiation and micrometeorite protection.

ICON engaged architecture firms BIG and SEArch+ to help design building typologies that could provide astronauts with safe, permanent accommodation on the lunar surface. The ring-shaped buildings developed by BIG feature waffled exteriors that provide both structure and protection protection from cosmic radiation, extreme temperatures and micro meteorite impacts. The ratio between internal volume and outer surface area is optimised to ensure the buildings can withstand the Moon's inhospitable environment and provide a comfortable indoor atmosphere.

ICON's 3D printer would operate autonomously, building dwelling units, landing pads and roads while being controlled remotely from a separate base or even from Earth. According to ICON co-founder and CEO, Jason Ballard, the Olympus Construction System is not just suited to lunar construction, but could also be used to solve housing challenges back on Earth by creating sustainable structures from indigenous materials.

← Four-storey semi-inflatable units could support a crew of four for up to 300 days at a time

Moon Village

Skidmore, Owings & Merrill + European Space Agency

The European Space Agency (ESA) has begun exploring the possibility of creating a permanent habitat on the Moon and has produced a design blueprint for what a lunar city might look like. US-based architecture firm Skidmore, Owings & Merrill (SOM) collaborated with ESA and faculty at the Massachusetts Institute of Technology to develop Moon Village – a self-sufficient settlement made up of semi-inflatable modules.

SOM based the design of the pressurised, four-level habitat modules on an existing structure used at the International Space Station. The design comprises a rigid composite frame and an inflatable structural shell that offers the optimal volume to mass ratio. Each module would accommodate four to six people and would allow for flexible interior arrangements. The modules would incorporate critical features including docking capability, life support systems, environmental control and radiation shielding.

Moon Village would be positioned at the South Polar region, where it would be able to harness sunlight energy thanks to the near-continuous daylight conditions. Food would be grown on site and the modules would be linked to enable seamless mobility throughout the settlement. Combining the modules in this way over time could enable the village to gradually grow into a city, with units dedicated to functions such as research, manufacturing, food culture and tourism. Although currently still a research project, Moon Village incorporates several innovations that will help ESA to fulfil its mission to shape the development of Europe's space capability.

← Each unit provides a net habitable volume of up to 390 cubic metres

← The modules can connect to form a larger settlement
↑ Units can be customised to suit research, manufacturing, food culture and tourism uses

Nüwa — ABIBOO Studio + SONet

Recent successful uncrewed missions to Mars have prompted more in-depth consideration of the possibility of colonising the Red Planet. International architecture firm ABIBOO Studio and scientific think-tank SONet developed this proposal for a self-sufficient and sustainable community on Mars that could house one million people.

The design comprises five cities, each accommodating between 200,000 and 250,000 people. The capital, Nüwa, would be built into a cliff face at a site called Tempe Mensa, where there is abundant access to water. The vertical city would consist of modular 'macro-buildings' embedded in the rock wall to protect inhabitants from radiation, meteorites and the planet's dangerously low atmospheric pressure. The standardised and scalable cylindrical structures would be organised into residential and work zones, connected by a three-dimensional network of tunnels.

The proposal seeks to address both the practical and emotional needs of humans living on Mars. Artificially created natural spaces called 'Green Domes' would function as parks and gardens incorporating familiar and experimental vegetation. A plateau at the top of the cliff would contain infrastructure dedicated to manufacturing, food production and energy generation, which would be automated due to the site's direct exposure to solar radiation. Domed pavilions in the valley below would provide recreational areas alongside hospitals, schools, universities and transportation connections to a space shuttle terminal. The city is intended to be built using local resources and would be able to sustain and grow itself in a sustainable manner following an initial phase of capital investment.

← A city built into the Martian cliffs protects inhabitants from radiation and meteorites

↑ Giant domes house amenities including public parks, hospitals and museums
↗ Spaces for living and working are connected by a three-dimensional network of tunnels

Planet City —— Liam Young

Liam Young is a speculative architect, designer and filmmaker whose work explores the ecological and technological consequences of creating and living in cities. Despite approaching his projects like a science-fiction author, Young's visions of future cities are largely built around existing technologies, such as drones, driverless cars and alternative energy sources.

One of his most radical proposals posits that all of humanity could be housed in a single giant metropolis built entirely from renewable resources over several generations. Planet City would be a self-sufficient, hyper-dense urban centre of ten billion people that would occupy just 0.02 per cent of the Earth's surface. This would allow rewilding to occur across the rest of the planet, restoring ecosystems previously damaged by humans.

The proposal was originally presented as a short film depicting 'residential mountains' rising up to 165 storeys tall, made from upcycled waste harvested from existing cities. Food would be grown in mega-farms and vertical orchards, with power supplied by solar panels and giant algae farms used to filter out pollution. As with most of Young's projects, Planet City is not intended as a blueprint for a future urban masterplan, but rather it is meant to provoke discussion about sustainability and the extreme measures that may be required to mend our broken world.

← Planet City imagines the entire human population living in a single hyper-dense metropolis

Credits

Front cover: Oceanix City by OCEANIX + BIG + Studio Other Spaces + UN-Habitat. Image © Bjarke Ingels Group

pp. 22 – 27 BiodiverCity Penang by BIG + Hijjas + Ramboll. Images © Bjarke Ingels Group / pp. 28 – 33 Port of Tallinn Masterplan by Zaha Hadid Architects. Images © Negativ VA, s.r.o. Courtesy of Zaha Hadid Architects / pp. 34 – 35 Nanjing Zendai Himalayas Center by MAD Architects. Photos by CreatAR Images © MAD Architects / pp. 36 – 37 Shenzhen Cultural District by MVRDV. Images © DACS 2021 / pp. 38 – 39 Liuzhou Forest City by Stefano Boeri Architetti. Images © Stefano Boeri Architetti / pp. 40 – 45 Oberbillwerder by ADEPT and Karres en Brands. Images © ADEPT + Karres en Brands / pp. 46 – 51 Jigna Eco-Community by Skidmore, Owings & Merrill. Images © Pixelflakes / pp. 58 – 59 New Deal Paris by Carlo Ratti Associati. Images © Carlo Ratti Associati / pp. 60 – 65 Ultra-Fast Charging Station for Electric Cars by Cobe and Clever. Images © Cobe and Rasmus Hjortshøj – COAST / pp. 66 – 71 EZ-PRO by Renault. Images by Julien Oppenheim © Renault Communication - Julien Oppenheim / pp. 72 – 73 Lilium Vertiports. Images © 2020-2021 Lilium GmbH / pp. 74 – 75 Airbus UAM by MVRDV + Airbus. Images © DACS 2021 / pp. 76 – 79 Uber Sky Tower by Pickard Chilton + ARUP. Images © Uber - Pickard Chilton - ARUP / pp. 80 – 81 Dragonfly by PriestmanGoode. Images © PriestmanGoode / pp. 82 – 83 Virgin Hyperloop. Images 1-2 © Virgin Hyperloop, Bjarke Ingels Group (BIG) and SeeThree; Image 3 © Virgin Hyperloop and Teague /pp. 84 – 85 Hardt Hyperloop Hub by UNStudio. Images © Plomp, courtesy of UNStudio / pp. 90 – 93 Self Sufficient City by WOHA. Images © WOHA / pp. 94 – 95 Pirelli 39 by Diller Scofidio + Renfro and Stefano Boeri Architetti. Images © Diller Scofidio + Renfro and Stefano Boeri Architetti / pp. 96 – 99 Toronto ORCA by Safdie Architects. Images © Safdie Architects / pp. 100 – 105 1Hotel Paris by Kengo Kuma & Associates. Images 1, 2, 4, 5 by Luxigon; Images 3, 6 by Mir. All images © Kengo Kuma & Associates / pp. 106 – 109 Southbank by Beulah, by UNStudio. Images © Norm Li, courtesy of UNStudio / pp. 110 – 113 Sunqiao Urban Agricultural District by Sasaki. Images © Sasaki / pp. 114 – 117 The Farmhouse by Precht. Images © Precht / pp. 118 – 119 Glasir by Framlab. Images © Framlab / pp. 124 – 127 BIOTIC by Carlo Ratti

Associati. Images © Carlo Ratti Associati / pp. 128 – 133 Woven City by Toyota + BIG. Images 1, 3, 4, 5, 6 © Bjarke Ingels Group; Image 2 © Squint Opera / pp. 134 – 135 Smart Forest City Cancun by Stefano Boeri Architetti. Images 1-2 © Stefano Boeri Architetti, Image 3 © The Big Picture / pp. 136 – 137 Blockchains City by Tom Wiscombe Architecture and EYRC Architects. Images © Tom Wiscombe Architecture / pp. 138 – 141 Brainport Smart District by UNStudio. Images 1, 3 © Plomp. Image 2 © UNStudio. All images courtesy of UNStudio / pp. 142 – 145 Konza Technopolis by SHoP Architects. Images © Konza Technopolis Development Authority / pp. 146 – 149 Milan Innovation District by Carlo Ratti Associati. Images © Carlo Ratti Associati / pp. 150 – 153 Berlin TXL Urban Tech Republic by Tegel Projekt GmbH and von Gerkan, Marg and Partners Architects. All images © gmp · von Gerkan, Marg and Partners Architects / pp. 154 – 155 Quayside by Sidewalk Labs and Waterfront Toronto. Images © Picture Plane for Heatherwick Studio for Sidewalk Labs / pp. 160 – 163 Oceanix City by OCEANIX + BIG + Studio Other Spaces + UN-Habitat. Images © Bjarke Ingels Group / pp. 164 – 165 Ocean Spiral by SHIMIZU CORPORATION. Images © SHIMIZU CORPORATION / pp. 166 – 169 Trenezia by Waugh Thistleton Architects. Images 1, 4 © Artec; Images 2, 3, 5 © Darcstudio. All images courtesy of Waugh Thistleton Architects / pp. 170 – 175 Re-defining Hong Kong's Waterfront by 10 Design. Images © 10 Design / pp. 176 – 177 City Sand by OXO Architectes. Images © Manal Rachdi OXO Architectes + NLA / pp. 178 – 179 Project Olympus by ICON + BIG + SEArch+. Images © Bjarke Ingels Group / pp. 180 – 183 Moon Village by Skidmore, Owings & Merrill + European Space Agency. Images © SOM | Slashcube GmbH / pp. 184 – 187 Nüwa by ABIBOO Studio + SONet. Images © ABIBOO Studio / pp. 188 – 189 Planet City by Liam Young. Images © Liam Young

Rear cover: Image 1; Self Sufficient City by WOHA. Image © WOHA / Image 2; Smart Forest City Cancun by Stefano Boeri Architetti. Image © Stefano Boeri Architetti

Concept
Alyn Griffiths

Texts
Ben van Berkel (foreword)
Alyn Griffiths

Copy editing
First Edition Translations

Book design
Tina Smedts – De Poedelfabriek

www.lannoo.com

Sign up to our newsletter for updates on our latest publications on art, interior design, food and travel, photography and fashion, as well as exclusive offers and events.

If you have any questions or comments about the material in this book, please do not hesitate to contact our editorial team: art@lannoo.com

D/2021/45/284 - NUR: 648/653
ISBN 9789401478588

- VLL - vermögenswirksame Leistungen
- 10% Leistungszulage
- Eversports · 54€ · 20 · 34€ von Brutto + hauseigene Kurse
- 25% Weihnachtsgeld
- Jobrad kündigen